HOW TO MAKE A
JAPANESE GARDEN

An inspirational visual guide to a classic garden style,
beautifully illustrated with over 80 stunning photographs

Charles Chesshire

HERMES
HOUSE

This edition is published by Hermes House,
an imprint of Anness Publishing Ltd
Hermes House
88–89 Blackfriars Road
London
SE1 8HA
tel. 020 7401 2077
fax 020 7633 9499

www.hermeshouse.com; www.annesspublishing.com

If you like the images in this book and would like to investigate using them for publishing, promotions or advertising, please visit our website www.practicalpictures.com for more information.

© Anness Publishing Ltd 2010

ETHICAL TRADING POLICY

At Anness Publishing we believe that business should be conducted in an ethical and ecologically sustainable way, with respect for the environment and a proper regard to the replacement of the natural resources we employ.

As a publisher, we use a lot of wood pulp to make high-quality paper for printing, and that wood commonly comes from spruce trees. We are therefore currently growing more than 750,000 trees in three Scottish forest plantations: Berrymoss (130 hectares/320 acres), West Touxhill (125 hectares/305 acres) and Deveron Forest (75 hectares/185 acres). The forests we manage contain more than 3.5 times the number of trees employed each year in making paper for the books we manufacture.

Because of this ongoing ecological investment programme, you, as our customer, can have the pleasure and reassurance of knowing that a tree is being cultivated on your behalf to naturally replace the materials used to make the book.

Our forestry programme is run in accordance with the UK Woodland Assurance Scheme (UKWAS) and will be certified by the internationally recognized Forest Stewardship Council (FSC). The FSC is a non-government organization dedicated to promoting responsible management of the world's forests. Certification ensures forests are managed in an environmentally sustainable and socially responsible way. For further information about this scheme, go to www.annesspublishing.com/trees

Material in this book previously appeared in *The Illustrated Encyclopedia of Japanese Gardening*.

Publisher: Joanna Lorenz
Senior Editors: Caroline Davison & Emma Clegg
Junior Editors: Joel Simons & Hannah Consterdine
Photographer: Alex Ramsay
Production Controller: Pirong Wang

PUBLISHER'S NOTE

Although the advice and information in this book are believed to be accurate and true at the time of going to press, neither the authors nor the publisher can accept any legal responsiblity or liability for any errors or omissions that may be made or for any resulting injury, damage or loss to persons or property as a result of carrying out any of the projects. Readers should follow all recommended safety procedures and wear the correct protective goggles, gloves and clothing.

NOTE TO READER

Each of the entries in the plant directory has been given a hardiness rating (for European readers) and a zone range (for readers in the United States):-

Hardiness Ratings

Frost tender Plant may be damaged by temperatures below 5°C (41°F).

Frost hardy Plant can withstand temperatures down to -5°C (23°F).

Half hardy Plant can withstand temperatures down to 0°C (32°F).

Fully hardy Plant can withstand temperatures down to -15°C (5°F).

Plant Hardiness Zones

The Agricultural Research Service of the U.S. Department of Agriculture has developed a system of plant hardiness zones. Every plant in the Directory section has been given a zone range. The zones 1–11 are based on the average annual minimum temperature. In the zone range, the smaller number indicates the northernmost zone in which a plant can survive the winter and the higher number gives the most southerly area in which it will perform consistently. Bear in mind that factors such as altitude, wind exposure, proximity to water, soil type, snow, night temperature, shade and the level of water received by a plant may alter a plant's hardiness by as much as two zones.

Zone 1 Below -45°C (-50°F)
Zone 2 -45 to -40°C (-50 to -40°F)
Zone 3 -40 to -34°C (-40 to -30°F)
Zone 4 -34 to -29°C (-30 to -20°F)
Zone 5 -29 to -23°C (-20 to -10°F)
Zone 6 -23 to -18°C (-10 to 0°F)
Zone 7 -18 to -12°C (0 to 10°F)
Zone 8 -12 to -7°C (10 to 20°F)
Zone 9 -7 to -1°C (20 to 30°F)
Zone 10 -1 to 4°C (30 to 40°F)
Zone 11 Above 4°C (40°F)

CONTENTS

Introduction

"Visualize the famous landscapes of our country and come to understand their most interesting points. Recreate the essence of these scenes in the garden, but do so interpretatively, not strictly."

From the Sakuteiki, the earliest known book of Japanese garden design, written in the 11th century

The Japanese garden has captured the imagination of Western gardeners ever since they discovered its delights in the 19th century. Japan, isolated from the rest of the world after the 1630s for over 200 years, had been nurturing extraordinary and unique styles of architecture, poetry, painting, flower arranging and gardening. Japanese garden design, in particular, exerted a powerful hold on those Western visitors.

It was the dynamic, creative energies of Zen monks and painters of the medieval period, alongside Japan's relationship with Chinese culture, that set the stage for the development of the Japanese garden. These ancient gardens have become the benchmark of abstract garden art throughout the world, and are unique demonstrations of the significance of water, plant and rock elements in the art of contemporary landscape gardening.

Japanese landscape gardens can be separated into five main styles – pond, dry, tea, stroll and courtyard – and each of these has a unique relationship with the history of Japan. Every element in the garden – plants, rocks, lanterns and water – plays a role in the creation of a unified, harmonious and poetic picture. Indeed, most of the plants used in Japanese gardens possess symbolic significance, including the twisted pine, scattered cherry blossom, pendulous wisteria, the lotus ('purity rising out of the mud') and fiery Japanese maple. These plants carefully placed with restraint and consideration, and gardeners celebrate the seasons through their fleeting beauty. Water is one of the most important elements in the Japanese garden. It can often be found in the form of a pond, stream or small water basin. Even when water is absent, its presence is symbolized through areas of sand and gravel, or dry streams. Rocks are equally important and are regarded as possessing a kind of spiritual and living essence that must be respected if they are to be placed successfully.

This book explores the art of the Japanese garden, tracking its development from the earliest garden of the Nara Period (710–94), through to modern and Western interpretations which combine the pure simplicity of Zen with contemporary landscaping materials. It examines the classic garden styles, pond, dry, tea, stroll and courtyard, and touches upon the variety of dry landscapes and *tsukubai* featured in Japanese garden design. The plant directory provides a selection of the unique flora of Japan and advises on seasonal highlights and care instructions.

Steeped in significance and refinement, the Japanese garden has enormous appeal, especially for garden designers seeking both a deeper meaning and a more contemporary edge. This book provides an inspirational introduction to the Japanese garden, a landscape in which the whole is far greater than the sum of its parts.

Right *A quintessential Japanese garden at Hosen-in, Ohara, where stepping stones traverse a serene pool.*

UNDERSTANDING THE JAPANESE GARDEN

The common Western impression of the Japanese Garden is of a small, carefully cultivated, stylized space, filled with clipped shrubs, rocks and stone artefacts such as lanterns, pagodas and Buddhas. In reality, the finest Japanese gardens are larger and more complex than many Western city gardens, and the artefacts are actually superfluous to their design. What counts is the spirit of the garden, and how the different elements are balanced. A sensitively styled Japanese garden should be created with naturalistic, asymmetric outlines and should recognize the power of *yugen* ("hidden depth") in colour, shade and light. This design principle has endured through numerous dramatic epochs in Japanese history, and the modern garden is a cultural symbol of unity between ancient and contemporary Japan.

Left *The roofline of the Great Buddha Temple of Nara is highlighted by the late evening sun. The view of the temple and the hills is "borrowed" by the garden of Isui-en to become part of the visual landscape.*

The evolution of the garden

There are six important periods in the history of the Japanese garden, most of them coinciding with dramatic changes in Japan's history. Each period is defined not only by the practicalities and customs of contemporary Japanese life, but also by the conflicts and changes brought about by religion, culture, politics and warfare.

Excavations in 1974 at Nara – the last of the ancient capitals of Japan – found vestiges of an ornamental garden on the site of an old palace. These gardens, dating back to 710, were quite similar to those that were constructed in China during the same period and are the earliest examples of Japanese garden design. The Nara period, as it became known, was followed by the Heian period (794–1185), the most romantic time in Japanese cultural history, which saw a great many

refinements in garden design, and also the writing of the *Sakuteiki*, possibly the world's first great garden treatise. One of the key features of this period was the creation of pond and island gardens that reproduced the Mystic Isles of the Immortals. The initial wave of Chinese influence was curtailed, however, by Minamoto, the first shogun (military dictator) of Japan, and it wasn't until Buddhist monks returned from China bearing artefacts of the Song dynasty that the shogun fully embraced Chinese arts. This resulted in the Kamakura Period (1185–1392), which saw the building of the Saiho-ji and Tenryu-ji gardens in Kyoto, both inspired by paintings of the Chinese Song dynasty.

The mingling of the warrior classes with the imperial classes in Kyoto during the subsequent Muromachi period (1393–1568) led to a further flowering of the arts.

Below *The gardens around Nijo castle, in Kyoto, were built at the beginning of the Edo period. These gardens used larger rocks than ever before and in greater numbers.*

Below *Zen monks created tea houses as places imbued with the spirirt of Zen, such as this one at Toji-in Temple, in Kyoto.*

Above *This contemporary design by Maureen Busby shows a strong interplay between the buildings and the gardens that surround them.*

Right *A garden of clipped shrubs* (o-karikomi), *at Sanzen-in, built during the Edo period. It is particularly renowned for its beautiful foliage.*

This epoch saw the building of the Golden Pavilion in the 1390s by Ashikaga shoguns, whose pond-filled stroll gardens were a departure from the earlier preference for boating lakes. The most important innovation of this period was the creation of "dry water" gardens – an innovation clearly influenced by Zen Buddhism that used rocks set in gravel or sand to symbolize water. From 1568, three successive military unifiers built gardens using far larger rocks than before, designed as an expression of power, but this excess was also tempered by the modesty of an important new feature: the tea house and garden. The famous tea-ceremony ritual was initially popularized by a merchant called Rikyu, one of the most influential figures in Japan; the ritual came to symbolize the Momoyama period, an era of the unifiers who would build Japan as a single nation.

Japan subsequently developed into a nation of isolation (1644–1911), a period signified by the private stroll gardens of Edo (now Tokyo); with its many pond-side tea houses and buildings, and exquisite framed views, it might represent the last great development in large-scale Japanese garden art. In time, gardens became more ostentatious, losing the creative edge and philosophical depth of their predecessors. Indeed, one of the latest movements in the evolution of the Japanese garden is toward a more natural style of garden design, featuring a combination of both native plantings and naturalistic streams. However, even the most modern gardens still refer back to the 11th-century Heian gardens in their use of natural materials, as was described in the oldest surviving work on Japanese gardening, the *Sakuteiki*.

Waves of influence

A whole host of outside influences were suddenly accessible to the Japanese people following their first contact with China in AD607. In Chinese gardens, islands were often used to represent the Mystic Isles, the mythical abode of the Immortals. These myths had a huge impact on the Japanese imagination and, to this day, the Mystic Isles still feature prominently. Buddhism also gained particular importance from the mid-7th century onwards, incorporating additional Chinese influences. Ponds were central to the Buddhist concept of paradise and became as essential to Japanese gardens as they had been in China: the great Amida garden of lakes and islands, for example, became the image for Nara and Heian-style gardens.

Toward the end of the 8th century, when the capital was moved to what is now Kyoto (Heian Kyo), the pond-and-winding-stream garden was the pre-eminent garden design. In fact, the choice of the site of the new city of Kyoto, modelled on the Chinese city of Chang'an and its palaces and gardens, followed Chinese geomantic principles. These principles affected the design of palaces, towns and gardens by their insistence that buildings, plants and rocks must be placed in a very precise manner to ensure that they were in balance and in tune with the natural order. Gradually, during the Heian period, fuelled by the cultured society of Kyoto and its new geomantic foundation, a true Japanese garden style began to emerge. This style slowly and indiscernibly blended Buddhism, the Mystic Isles and Shinto's sacred groves into the distinctive art form so recognizable today.

The subsequent wave of influences on the Japanese garden (as well as the Japanese tea house and eventually the tea garden) also came from China, in part through its painters. Japanese monks, meanwhile, found in China practitioners of Chan (or Zen, as it is known in Japan), a word derived from the Sanskrit *dyana*, which means meditation. By the late 1500s, Japanese Zen masters had become the next great garden-makers, once again inspired by Chinese and Japanese paintings featuring dry gardens of sand and rocks.

Following its enforced reconnection with the West towards the end of the 19th century, Japan showed an extraordinary capacity to assimilate and influence other traditions. Indeed, the Zen-style garden influenced many Western designers, who found in the garden an art form that gave expression to their own minimalist and avant-garde creations. In Japan there was (and still is) a hunger for English-style gardens, which were initially reproduced, just as Chinese gardens had been, before being integrated into the Japanese mainstream and given a Japanese slant.

By the early 20th century, however, the design of more traditional Japanese gardens had become rather stale and clichéd, and this situation prompted designers to re-evaluate the use of established materials and motifs. More recently, many newly created gardens have replaced natural rocks and boulders with raw, blasted, quarried materials in much the same way as 17th-century gardens blended the artificial with the natural. This incorporation of new materials, while retaining the pure simplicity of Zen gardens, is the hallmark of contemporary Japanese garden design.

Opposite *The raked circles of sand or gravel represent the eight rough seas; the hills of moss, the five sacred mountains; and the rocks, islands – together telling the story of the Mystic Isles of the Immortals.*

The natural landscape

Looking out over an expanse of sand raked into perfect lines, set in a perfect rectangular courtyard with one or two rocks, and an azalea or two clipped so much that they barely flower, you might be forgiven for thinking that Japanese gardeners are more inclined to fly in the face of nature than sympathize with it. Yet Japan's own natural landscape of mountains, windswept pines, waterfalls and islands directly inspires and informs their garden designs, resulting in a spiritual style that gives inspiration to gardeners all over the world.

A mountainous archipelago of four main islands, Japan also has hundreds of small rocky islets. The mountains – over 50 of which are volcanic – are steep and wooded and scored with rocky streams, hot springs and rivers. In fact, most are still wooded up to their peaks because, until recently, Buddhism was the official religion and the eating of meat and fish was prohibited. This meant that, unlike in other parts of the world, their hills and mountains have not been stripped of vegetation by sheep, goats and cattle.

To this day, natural features such as mountains, rocks and streams inspire Japanese garden designers and are recurring features of the Japanese garden. The natural mountainous and coastal landscapes of Japan, and people's spiritual reverence for rocks and trees through ancient religions such as Shinto, exert a powerful influence on design, alongside the more ancient Chinese themes. By incorporating a careful selection of indigenous plants and imitating the natural features of the countryside, albeit in a restrained, stylized form, Japanese garden designers have developed a unique style befitting a truly enigmatic natural landscape.

Below *The arrangement of the rocks and the pruning of the trees at Syoko-ho-en could lead one to believe they are in the mountains instead of in the middle of Kyoto.*

Above *The azaleas in the garden of Murin-an are clipped into abstract, enigmatic shapes and dispersed randomly in a mountainous landscape design.*

Right *The first appearance of cherry blossom is celebrated up and down Japan as a symbol of spring. Ornamental cherry trees have been planted in Japan since the Heian period.*

Left *In the garden of Syoko-ho-en, Kyoto, the placement of the rocks and the pruning of the trees and shrubs follow the "desires" of nature. In the foreground, the autumn-flowering toad lily (Tricyrtis) grows near the edge of the stream.*

Architectural elements

The relationship between a Japanese garden and the architecture of the main house, temple or garden buildings is quite unlike that of the formal Western garden. In the West, the details and forms of the architecture tend to influence the design of formal gardens, but by contrast the formal Japanese garden enjoys the interplay between the angularity of the architecture and the curve of natural forms. Although dry and courtyard gardens are often contained within the rectilinear confines of garden walls, the gardens themselves are more like paintings viewed within a picture frame. In other styles of Japanese garden, the natural forms of stepping stones, rocks, pine boughs and bamboos are brought very close to the buildings. Sometimes camellias or azaleas may be clipped into

geometric forms to accentuate or even imitate the architecture, but asymmetry and dynamic natural forms within the design are usually preferred.

The Japanese buildings of the Nara (710–94) and Heian (794–1185) periods, like their gardens, were more or less copies of Chinese ones. But differences began to develop during the Heian period: the Japanese already showed a preference for the natural finish of timber, rather than the more flamboyant painted buildings common in China at the time, and roofs were also less sweeping and curved than their Chinese counterparts. The centrepiece of Heian aristocratic homes was known as the *shinden* ("sleeping hall") which had two adjacent wings connected by corridors; in the space between these two corridors was an open, sand-covered

Below *The layout of the garden at Shoden-ji can be viewed from the veranda of the temple, drawing in the sacred mountain of Mount Hiei.*

Below *In the dry garden at the Tofuku-ji, the lines of raked sand make it hard to define exactly where the building ends and the garden begins.*

courtyard which was reserved for ceremonies and entertainment. Through part of this courtyard, a stream might meander and feed into the main pond beyond.

Over the next 200 years, Japanese architecture evolved into smaller and more refined urban residences. By the Muromachi period (1393–1568), monks and samurai showed a marked preference for the *shoin* style. *Shoin* was a term that referred to the alcove that was set within one of the outer walls of the main building. This alcove had papered walls in order to allow natural light to illuminate a specially designed shelf or a desk for reading and writing. This new architectural style was used in many temples and houses, which also had verandas and sliding panels that opened up to reveal their gardens.

The tea house also employed some aspects of the *shoin* style, especially the alcove, but the general style of tea-house architecture was more rustic. The Japanese style of tea house, which was originally known as the "mountain place in the city", combined the rustic charm of the thatched hut (*soan*) with the sophistication of a more literary and urban style of architecture (*shoin*). This hybrid style was, and still is, the most popular for building tea houses and garden buildings.

The art of framing a landscape is even more important to Japanese garden design. This technique is called *shakkei*, or "borrowed scenery", but was once known by the more evocative term *ikedori*, meaning "captured alive". *Shakkei* meant that prominent distant features could, in effect, be drawn into the garden itself and so become an intrinsic part of its overall composition.

Above right *The pillars on the verandas of temples and tea houses can frame the garden beyond them.*

Right *Sliding rice paper panel doors (*shoji*) open up a view from a tatami-matted tea room at Isui-en, Nara. The geometric lines interact with the weaving branches.*

CLASSIC GARDEN STYLES

The various styles of Japanese garden have evolved for over a millennium. During that time, there have been dramatic cultural and historic changes that have clearly helped to create a few very distinctive styles. This section introduces and examines the typical features of each garden style. It explores the tranquillity, joy and serenity of the pond and stream gardens, the "dry mountain water" of the dry garden, the ancient philosophy of the tea garden, and the unique simplicity of the stroll garden. Detailing the distinct features of each, as well as their interlinking histories, this chapter offers an introduction to the Japanese garden as a place for perpetuating the ancient myths of immortality, and celebrating plants, flowers and the changing of the seasons.

Left *The formality of this path cutting through the dry garden of Tenju-an is softened by an enveloping carpet of moss.*

Pond gardens

Ponds, lakes and streams have always been central to the Japanese garden, instilling a sense of tranquillity, joy and calm. Water features, such as ponds and streams, usually appear totally natural within the surrounding landscape, even if they are constructed artificially, and obvious manmade features, such as fountains, are avoided. Following the emperor's restoration as head of state between the 17th and 19th centuries, gardens were created to reawaken the spirit of earlier periods. Such a naturalistic aesthetic becomes all the more relevant in times when nature is so much under threat, especially in Japan.

We can gain some inspiration for the design of present-day pond gardens by looking briefly at a famous example from Japan's past, Motsu-ji, in Hiraizumi, Iwate, which is one of the very few surviving pond and island gardens from the 12th century. Today, you can still see Motsu-ji's great lake, which is bordered by formal iris beds and dramatic rock arrangements. The

lakes of early pond gardens such as Motsu-ji were broad and well lit, glimmering under the sun, moon and stars, while weeping willows swayed and shaded their banks. This style of pond garden differs from the later stroll gardens in having none of the more familiar tea houses, lanterns or water basins. Instead, the pond contained islands, often linked by bridges.

Pond gardens remained popular in Japan, but as they became smaller, their outline grew increasingly complex and indented and the rock arrangements more artistic and painterly. The sumptuous gowns of the ladies of the Heian period would have made it impossible for them to stroll around large lakeside gardens, and so in the Kamakura and Muromachi periods, ponds became smaller, and formed part of the first real stroll gardens, a style of Japanese garden that we will look at later on. Most of these later pond and stream gardens were confined within walls, which meant that their size was fairly limited – a factor that makes it easier for us to envisage the practicalities of trying to create one in a smaller Western garden. While later gardens were influenced by painters and Zen philosophy, the Heian pond garden simply uses nature as a principal feature in the design.

The *Sakuteiki*, which was written in the Heian period, names many forms of pond styles, islands, streams and waterfalls, and even notes the best techniques for planting trees. In Japan, inanimate rocks were, and still are, thought to possess personalities that must be treated with respect. This interplay between the formality of the surrounding architecture and the informality of the garden is part of the genius of Japanese garden design.

Above *Waterfalls and pond inlets in pond gardens are built with naturalism and artistry.*

Right *This stepping-stone bridge in the garden of Tenju-an is made of unusually shaped piers, possibly recycled temple-pillar bases. These bridges zig-zag across the water to offer a variety of views.*

Opposite *An ambitious waterfall scheme in the Rheinaue, Germany, creates drama through well-observed rock arrangements and in the ways that the water spills over the rocks.*

Another common feature of the pond garden was the group of islands that represented the Isles of the Immortals. Some of these took the form of turtles and cranes. They can be included in today's gardens, although it is important to point out that Japanese representations of the crane or turtle are rarely naturalistic. The crane island is made up of a group of rocks, with one taller rock usually sitting up like a wing. In the groups of rocks representing turtles, the head and flippers are sometimes discernible, but more often the image is utterly abstract and only a trained eye can appreciate what is being depicted.

Turtle and crane motifs are not essential to a pond garden but can be included if they are treated with sensitivity. Similarly, a pine island is evocative of the windswept pine-clad islands of Matsushima, a scenic site in northern Japan, famous throughout Japanese garden history. Large pond gardens may include several pine islands of varying sizes, which could be reached by a traditional Chinese red-painted bridge, the most popular style when Matsushima was built.

The pond garden style

The pond will, naturally, be the central feature, and should ideally be big enough for you to incorporate an island or two, and, for greater authenticity, to make a ride in a small rowing boat possible. For this you will need space – it is obviously not suitable for a small town garden – as well as the time and energy to plan on a large scale. The edges of the pond should have a varied and natural outline resembling a coastline, with coves, grotto-like caves and beaches. Rocks can be placed at the edges of ponds and by waterfalls so long as their shape is considered carefully, and also in the water, where they can be used as stepping stones or supports for naturalistic bridges.

There are many accompanying styles of island to choose from, but the most popular is the pine island, planted with one very picturesque pine, or a group of pines set in a tight group. In pond gardens the island is often reached by a bridge, especially an old-style Chinese wooden bridge that is painted red or orange.

Left *Chinese-style red-painted bridges, such as this one at the Tully Japanese Garden in Ireland, were popular in the early days of Japanese gardens of the Heian period. They were also used extensively in the later Edo gardens.*

Opposite *The 700-year-old pond in the garden of Tenju-an, with its simple design of two ponds, two islands and rock arrangements around a waterfall. Ponds were originally used for boating parties for poetry readings, chanting and music. As ponds became smaller, as here, strolling took over from boating.*

You may of course prefer a different style of bridge, perhaps aiming for a more minimal, neutral effect. Another typical feature of a pond garden is a winding stream that either feeds into or empties the main pond (or both). This would originally have been used for ceremonial purposes, but even without the ceremonies it makes an attractive addition. Again it should follow a naturalistic course, and be planted at its edges with hostas and other waterside plants. Indeed, planting in pond gardens should be in naturalistic groups of trees and shrubs that celebrate the seasons. Groves of cherries, maples and pines can be underplanted with azaleas, kerria and spiraea for contrast. A strolling path is the final essential feature that should be added, in order to encourage the visitor to experience every part of the garden by wandering around the pond and over the stream.

Typical features of a pond garden:
• a pond with rocks around the edges and cobble and sandy beaches shelving into the water;

• one or two islands, typically planted with pines and grasses among rocks;

• a red-painted Chinese-style bridge;

• a meandering stream or waterfall feeding the pond;

• undulating hills around the pond;

• plants such as cherry trees, Japanese maples, kerria, azalea and spiraea.

Dry gardens

Dry gardens are often referred to as *kare-sansui*, which literally means "dry mountain water". In this type of garden, water is replaced by sand, gravel or pebbles, making the dry garden synonymous with the more commonly known Zen garden. References to such dry landscapes occur as early as the 11th century, but they refer to the natural placement of rocks in grass or moss, and not to dry representations of water. Possible origins include the great shrines at Ise that stand in vast rectangles of gravel, and Joeji-in, near Yamaguchi, where a collection of rocks was laid in an area of moss between the temple and the pond. This garden, created in the mid-1400s, is attributed to Sesshu, the great Japanese painter, who reproduced his brush strokes in the garden using flat-topped and angular rocks.

These dry gardens were not created because of a natural absence of water. Instead, they were made for a mixture of artistic and philosophical reasons. Artistically, the dry garden was based on the works of Japanese painters, whose art inspired gardeners to use a monochromatic treatment of the landscape. Such designs were also linked to the philosopical teachings of Zen.

The Ryoan-ji garden in Kyoto is a timeless example of the exceptional degree of artistry shown by the garden makers of the late 15th century, when it is

Below *The rocks in this area of the garden at Nanzen-ji in Kyoto are arranged to display their innate quality in the most artistic way.*

thought this garden was constructed. It is also a fine representation of the influence of Zen and Buddhism seen in gardens of this style.

The Ryoan-ji is a rectangular courtyard bordered on three sides by a clay and oil wall and by the abbot's quarters on the fourth, where a long veranda overlooks the garden from a higher level of around 75cm (30in). The area is about the size of a tennis court, and is neatly edged in a frame of blue-grey tiles. The whole of the inner space is spread with a fine, silvery grey quartzite grit that is raked daily along its length in parallel lines. This "sea" of sand is the background canvas to 15 rocks in five groups of 5-2-3-2-3, fringed by moss. This pattern recurs throughout the Far East, even in the rhythm of music and the chanting of Buddhist texts. The parallel lines of raked gravel break their pattern and form circles around the groups of rocks like waves lapping against island shores. The magical way that the rocks are grouped and spaced has gripped generations of visitors.

No one knows the exact meaning of these groupings. Some have described them as a tiger taking her cubs across a river, while others see them as mountains in the mist or as islands surrounded by sea. Whatever the rationale, Ryoan-ji is one of the great examples of a dry garden governed by both artistic and philosophical principles.

Above right *The dry garden at Ryoan-ji was first laid out in 1449. The composition of 15 rocks is set in a rectangle of sand, against a backdrop of an oil and clay wall overhung with trees. The raked circles of sand represent the rough seas and the rocks the sacred mountains of the Mystic Isles.*

Right *The Mystic Isles rock arrangement at Tofuku-ji has immense power. The designer, Mirei Shigemori, used much larger and darker rocks than was traditional.*

The Influence of Zen

Most dry gardens appear in Zen temples and are therefore strongly associated with Zen Buddhism. They can be viewed as paintings, illustrating idealized landscapes "hung" within their rectangular frame. In Zen, through meditation, one can experience what is known as the "void"; this "meditative void" – which Zen defines as the original human state – can be equated to the empty space of raked sand in a dry garden. While lay people might look at a Zen garden and see mountaintops circled in mist, practitioners of Zen will simply see a reflection of the infinite space that lies deep within us. The act of raking gravel is a meditative practice for Zen Buddhist monks and some Zen gardens include arrangements of rocks for monks to contemplate that signify aspects of Buddhism.

The dry garden style

In the intial stages of planning a dry garden, first imagine a distant misty mountain landscape, a stream with waterfalls or a rocky shoreline. Look at how streams and rivers flow, how waves lap against rocks, and you will learn to use the inspiration of nature to make raked gravel patterns around rocks. Once you have composed a picture in your mind, then let go of the superfluous and simply allow the essence of the composition to take over, and minimize it. Remember that an unfilled space is just as important as a space containing objects or plants. This "minimalism" has inspired many contemporary garden designers to reproduce the dry garden in modern urban environments. After all, dry gardens were often created in domestic courtyards, not just in Zen temples. A simple composition could be created with a rock or two, a stone lantern, a water basin and a section of bamboo fence set in a stretch of sand.

Left *The garden of Tenju-en, Kyoto, is an example of the interplay between geometric manmade and irregular natural forms.*

Opposite left *At Nanzen-ji, in Kyoto, over two-thirds of the dry garden is composed of sand. The rest is dedicated to this group of rocks and shrubs.*

Opposite right *Dry rock arrangements are often centred around a main stone, which may symbolize the Buddha, the sacred mountain of Shimesen or Mount Horai of the Mystic Isles. This can be seen in the dry garden at Ryogen-in, created in the 1980s, where the mountainous island of Horai is represented by the central stone.*

Before you start you must have a good idea of the elements you want to introduce and be certain that you can get all of them to the site. Rocks are especially difficult to move in narrow confines, but mini-diggers can get through openings of around 1m (1yd) wide, which might be sufficient. If you are contemplating growing plants in your dry garden, make sure the soil is right for them. If there is no soil on site or the drainage is poor, you can build up planting areas between rock arrangements or dig trenches to improve the drainage. The first priority is to get the rocks in place as this will be the most awkward and messy job. After this, you can frame your "picture" with edging stones that will contain the area of gravel and will set off both the gravel and the rocks. The Zen quality of a dry garden is more effectively achieved by the creation of elements for both casual viewing and contemplation.

Typical features of a pond garden:

• a rectangle of edging stones or tiles to frame the garden;

• rocks of interesting shapes;

• gravel, preferably light or silvery grey;

• moss around the bases of rocks to make them look like islands;

• stepping stones and lanterns;

• bent pines and small-leaved evergreens to tuck around the rocks;

• clipped azaleas to imitate hills.

Tea gardens

Tea gardens are designed as places in which to appreciate *sado*, the tea-drinking ceremony, which conventionally begins in the outer half of the tea garden, known as the outer *roji*. Guests are then led deeper into the garden to the tea house. On the way, they might pass through a middle "stooping gate", perhaps with a lantern nearby, designed to force the guests to bow slightly – a moment of enforced humility to stimulate an awareness of the material world the guests are leaving behind. After passing under the stooping gate, the guests enter the inner *roji* that surround the tea house. This part of the garden is the "wilderness", which represents the wild mountain landscape that might surround a Chinese hermitage. The guests then wash their hands and mouths at a low basin called a *tsukubai* (or "stooping basin"). This is a lower style of basin than the taller *chozubachi*, which is a water basin more frequently found near the veranda of the main house. After cleansing themselves, the guests proceed to the tea house, remove their shoes and enter through a small hatch-like entrance, the *nigiriguchi*. Once inside, the guests might admire a seasonal flower arrangement and a scroll hanging in an alcove, known as the *tokonoma*. Such gardens and houses were seen to represent a break in a journey from a busy urban centre to a secluded country retreat.

Tea was originally drunk by Buddhist monks as an aid to wakefulness during their long hours of meditation. Buddhist monks thus brought Zen Buddhism, poetry, fine porcelain and art appreciation together by creating what is known as the "tea ceremony", drawing the simple act of drinking tea into the realm of high art. By the mid-16th century, tea ceremonies, tea houses and tea gardens were part of the culture of Japan, exemplified by the "mountain places in the city", an evolution of tea houses built in the back gardens of cities such as Kyoto, Nara and the port of Sakai, near present-day Osaka. Such gardens were originally based on paths, symbolizing the routes taken by pilgrims on their way to meet sages in their hermitages. The tea garden, or *roji*, which means "dewy path" or "dewy ground", evokes those mountain paths and gradually evolved to include an elaborate set of sophisticated symbols. By the 17th century, tea paths were often made of formal square paving and millstones, while tea houses also evolved, becoming more refined, more open and less humble.

Left *The most important feature of the tea garden is the path and gateway that leads to the tea house, which opens into the environs of the tea house itself.*

Opposite *The veranda pillars at Hosen-in frame the scene from the tea house. The Japanese white pine could be over 700 years old.*

Later still, tea houses changed into tea arbours, where tea might be drunk while looking out over the garden. The changing aesthetic from the Muromachi period through to the Edo period shows a slow evolution from *wabi-sabi* ("withered loneliness"), indicating a taste for the impoverished, to *asobi*, a more playful and artistic style.

The tea house was often built to look like a rustic thatched hut, although it was always constructed with the finest planed timber. The rustic appearance of the tea house, combined with the refinement of domestic and temple architecture, created a whole new language in garden architecture – a discipline that is still studied today. A tea garden can include a range of decorative features, such as gates, water basins and lanterns, as well as following certain aesthetic rules, such as an attention to detail and cleanliness, which are apparent in all Japanese gardens.

In small town gardens where space may not allow for a tea house, the Japanese will convert one room in the house into a tea room with a tatami-matted floor. For the tea garden they would still devise a path, or *roji*, that wanders through a "wilderness" of just a few paces from one door, then returning via a side door, perhaps with a *nigiriguchi*, into the tea room. The whole point is to be able to create an illusion of wandering across a wild mountainside. The onus is placed on the guests to comprehend that the journey they are taking is "real", but to help them, the garden designer will often include pointers and hints as to the symbolic nature of each element. If a whole *roji* is reduced to only a few metres in length, it would still include a few stepping stones, a water basin, a lantern and one or two plants, such as a camellia or a bamboo, to suggest the wilderness. A rock might indicate a mountain, while a post might be enough to suggest a middle crawl-through gate. That is the essence of the tea garden: creating a spiritual, rather than a literal, journey.

The tea garden style

Once the significance of the tea garden has been grasped, you can be as creative as you want, just like the designers of the 16th century. While one tea master might have enjoyed a natural look, another might have preferred a creative mix of the manmade and the natural. Such adaptability is the main reason why tea houses and tea gardens never really died out, reappearing in stroll gardens and courtyard gardens to the present.

A tea garden does not have to be imbued with the tenets of Zen to be intriguing or even beautiful. Indeed, when Zen Buddhism went out of favour in Japan and Confucianism was in the ascendancy, the tea ceremony continued to thrive, but it evolved to express a more outward and cultured refinement than the deeper inner transformative power of Zen. This illustrates just how flexible the concept of the tea ceremony and garden can be, and that it can easily be reinterpreted to accommodate virtually any culture. When you are creating a tea garden of your own, you could make a simple layout with just a few scattered rocks, bamboos, natural paving and bamboo gates, or a much more elaborate affair. You could build your own tea house, to whatever level of complexity and authenticity you want, or you could simply convert any garden building into a tea house, even with chairs and tables, although the space should be kept clean and treated with a certain degree of reverence, so that you can entertain guests in a quiet and respectful atmosphere. All you really need for a tea garden is a path.

Right *A stone pathway leads to the entrance of a tea garden.*

Opposite *A special lacquered table is prepared for an outdoor tea ceremony* (no-da-te)*, often conducted in an informal style.*

Typical features of a tea garden:

• an entrance gate;

• a winding stepping-stone path;

• a water basin with cobbles around it;

• lanterns to light the path and basin;

• a waiting room or bench for guests ;

• a middle crawl-through gate;

• woodland planting of camellias, maples and bamboos, and low planting of ferns and sedges around rocks.

Stroll gardens

A stroll garden is one in which the visitor is encouraged to amble slowly along paths that circle around a small pond or lake. It is one of the most familiar Japanese garden styles, partly because it incorporates so many aspects of other styles. You will find stepping-stone paths, lanterns, water basins and tea houses from the tea garden; expanses of sand with a rock or two, usually near the main building, from the dry garden; and the use of water in streams, waterfalls and ponds from the pond garden. Other elements might include bamboo fences and bridges of all kinds. The tea houses, tea arbours, lanterns, bridges and contrived views of scenes reproduced from historic or famous places around Japan or even China were all carefully placed to entertain the stroller.

When the stroll garden was developed in the 17th century, the pervasive aesthetic of the times was not as "spiritual" as that of the earlier dry and tea gardens. There was more of a sense of playfulness (*asobi*) as well as a desire for the sumptuous and magnificent, and Japanese garden owners prided themselves on their connoisseurship of the arts.

Nevertheless, stroll gardens managed not to be overly ostentatious because they still employed the restraint and cultivated poverty of many of the aspects of the tea garden. This restraint in garden design was known as *shibumi* (meaning "astringent"), which underlined their markedly minimalist, unpretentious and subdued beauty. A stroll garden could be as large as 20 hectares (50 acres) or be created in as little as 25sq m (about a sixteenth of an acre). Through the careful use of space and meandering paths, smaller areas can be made to look much larger than they actually are. One device that was commonly practised in stroll gardens was the "borrowing" of scenery, such as distant buildings and hills outside the bounds of the garden, as part of the garden plan – a technique known as *shakkei*.

In most stroll gardens, rocks played a far less prominent role than they had in the earlier Kamakura and Muromachi periods, partly because the Edo period

Opposite *A stream enters a pool at Murin-an, in Kyoto, a late 19th-century stroll garden.*

Left *A mass of clipped azaleas is typical of the planting style in Edo period stroll gardens. A few rocks are interspersed among them, but rocks generally feature less prominently than in earlier styles.*

was based on the new capital, Edo (Tokyo), where rocks were far scarcer than they had been around the previous capital, Kyoto. In certain stroll gardens, however, rocks were sometimes sparsely used to symbolize the great power of the shogun. The scarcity of rocks led garden designers to rely more on clipped shrubs for dramatic form. This distinctive form of topiary, known as *o-karikomi*, is a fine art that is still practised extensively today.

Although stroll gardens are designed to be walked around, they are also meant to be viewed from the main house or from arbours in the garden. Traditional Japanese houses had verandas, raised above ground level, from which you look over an expanse of brushed or raked sand stretching as far as the pond. At the near edge of the pond you will find clipped azaleas and an occasional rock. Distant shores might be overhung by pines, their branches supported by posts.

At one end of the pond, a stream might enter, with a wide estuary traversed with stepping stones. These may be made from natural stone or formal slabs. Bridges that cross over streams or inlets can be a single slab of curved, carved granite, or a curved wooden bridge, sometimes painted red like a Chinese bridge. In more naturalistic settings, log bridges or natural stone can be used. The stream babbles over pebbles as it enters the pond. Further upstream, it is narrower, tumbling between rocks and over waterfalls, and hugged by ferns and sedges. Even though stroll gardens may lack the spirituality of other styles, they obey certain rules of balance, and look to nature or famous scenes for their inspiration.

Right *An early Edo period stroll garden in Kyoto. Here the rocks are dramatic and symbolic of the power of the Shogun Tokugwa Ieyasu, who built this garden at Nijo Castle.*

The stroll garden style

Developed as a way to combine many aspects of the tea garden, dry garden and pond garden, the central feature of a stroll garden is usually a pond, with a gravel path that weaves around it, taking in views of specially composed scenes. Stroll gardens can range dramatically in size from park-like gardens to relatively small spaces; in small gardens, it may be possible to increase the sense of space using the technique of *shakkei* (borrowed view or scenery).

To plan a stroll garden you need some kind of vision of a scenic landscape so that you can sketch out the general contours and outline of the pond. From the house you may also compose a scene that will be framed by a window or an arbour. In a stroll garden you may have some open grassy areas, some hills, a bridge and one or two good vantage points from where a variety of scenes can be viewed. Ponds should have some shady, deeper areas for fish to

shelter from the heat. Paths can be made in any style but the main strolling path should be surfaced in gravel and wide enough for two people to be able to stroll side by side. The main challenge when creating a stroll garden is how to keep the pond water healthy. Unless you are lucky enough to have a natural stream, you will need to circulate the water with a pump, otherwise you might have a stagnant, half-empty pond by midsummer. You should also make sure that your site is large enough to spread out the soil that is removed when you dig out the pond. This soil can be used to construct small hills, making the site more interesting and intriguing for people using the main gravelled path to wander around visiting tea houses and arbours. Any fairly open site with good soil, some sunshine and good access can be used. Shady areas can be adapted to grow azaleas and hydrangeas, but cherry trees need an open aspect in order to grow and flower well.

Typical features of a stroll garden:

- a pond;

- a stream and cascade or waterfall;

- stone or wooden bridges over the stream or to an island on the pond;

- rocks among the plants at the pond edge;

- small hills with dwarf or pruned pines;

- a strolling path in gravel or paving stones;

- gates into the tea garden;

- stepping-stone or paved tea paths;

- a wisteria arbour;

- a waiting room or bench;

- a tea house or tea arbour for viewing;

- fences surrounding the garden and bordering the tea path;

- *shakkei*, or "borrowed scenery";

- lanterns and water basins near the tea house;

- extensive plantings including: groves of cherries, plums and maples; groups of clipped azaleas, bamboo and hydrangeas; evergreen trees and herbaceous plants such as grasses and anemones.

Left *Although generally they are more elaborate and impressive, stroll gardens often include features found in earlier pond gardens, such as the stone bridge here.*

Courtyard gardens

The history of the courtyard garden starts in the early 17th century, but for contemporary designers the small, enclosed space adjoining a building still offers fantastic design possibilities. Courtyard gardens are generally simple, sometimes planned as an extension of the house with large windows and doors, sometimes as a functional outdoor space. Small courtyard gardens, designed to be viewed through glass panels or set within atriums open to the sky, are now being created everywhere from large museums and corporate headquarters to private homes.

In the Heian period, courtyard gardens, or tsubos, were small enclosed spaces with perhaps a single plant. During the Edo period, merchants amassed great wealth but were still the lowest class in society, and thus this wealth could be confiscated. As a result, the merchants developed a domestic architecture of room complexes and enclosed courtyards, known as *machiya*, behind an unassuming shopfront. These courtyards borrowed design elements and features from earlier garden styles without necessarily following the guiding principles and religious philosophies that shaped them.

Some of these Edo-period courtyard gardens or tsubo-niwas can still be seen in cities throughout Japan. The courtyard garden style is once again rising in popularity, although this is as a result of space constraints rather than a need for concealment.

Above *Bamboo fence posts are frequently used in courtyard gardens to deflect or to help frame a view.*

Left *Dry gardens can give surprising life to inner courtyards where few plants would grow. The great waves of sand add a sense of movement in this garden at Ryogen-in.*

In addition to their aesthetic appeal, minuscule courtyard gardens perform the important role of bringing light and air into the home, while the verandas running around their edges join together the *machiya's* various areas. Though tiny in scale, the quality of the garden's lanterns, rocks and other components were and still are clear indicators of the taste and affluence of the *machiya's* occupants. Through the use of sliding screens, fence panels and bamboo blinds, it is possible to view these internal gardens from different angles, with each aspect framed within the rectilinear bounds of doors and window frames. The distinction between indoors and outdoors disappears. Westerners who explored Japan in the mid-19th century were astonished by the stroll gardens, but were equally amazed by these beautiful small town gardens. Due to the enclosure of many *machiya*, such gardens were invariably too shady and too small for most flowering shrubs or cherries, limiting foliage choices to glossy evergreen shrubs such as aucubas, fatsias and camellias, as well as shade-loving ferns, bamboos and farfugiums. There is also often a carpeting of moss, just as would have been found in a traditional tea garden with its shady walks and scattered rocks.

In many ways, the courtyard style – a hybrid of the dry garden and the tea garden – suits the modern world well, and is often highly refined. Some of these gardens have everything from lanterns, water basins, small bridges, gravel and rocks to shady plants and sections of fencing used as a partition or to create privacy. Courtyard gardens are often interpreted in a minimalist style today, maybe consisting simply of a single clump of bamboo planted off-centre or a group of rocks with ferns and moss. In fact the courtyard garden is an ideal medium for the contemporary garden designer, as the minimalist style is now so popular. Roof gardens can also be classified as courtyard

Above *Stepping stones across sand look effective when surrounded by moss. In a house with no separate tea-garden, guests would perhaps leave the house by one door, and walk along the path to enter by another door.*

gardens, even though they may include views over the outside world. The raw, open, soil-less space on top of a building is perfect for the dry-landscape treatment, particularly where there are worries that excess weight from plants, pots, soil and water might damage the building's structure. The use of sand, lightweight plants and even fibreglass rocks in the Japanese style is often the best solution for a roof garden.

The courtyard garden style

A courtyard garden is any small area in an enclosed space that incorporates traditional features found in other Japanese garden styles. Some are dry gardens with just a spread of sand and one or two rocks, while others might include elaborate paths that cross over the space, using plantings that evoke a distant but miniaturized landscape. A courtyard garden requires careful design. If you want to include a number of features, then you must have an overall composition that is coherent. Consider whether your garden is going to act as a path from one room to another, or is simply going to be viewed from one or two points. There is also a question of scale. A *shakkei*, or condensed landscape, for example, should not have too many features, as this might make it appear too busy. Make a plan, and stand back from time to time to check the view over the garden as you construct it.

Opposite *This tiny garden at Sanzen-in is a welcome island of green in the centre of the building, with enough light for plants such as ferns and bamboos to grow.*

Below *Two water basins* (chozubachi) *that can be reached from the veranda of Sanzen-in, in Ohara. These types are square basins set on stone pillars.*

As courtyards are, by their very nature, enclosed, access to them can be tricky, so make sure you can get all the materials into the space (some may have to come through the house, which could be difficult). Also, being so close to a house, the space may have water, electricity and gas services crossing underneath, so check before doing any excavation. Generally, deep excavation is not necessary in courtyard gardens except to ensure that the site is well drained before planting anything. Courtyards may not have a great deal of light, so plants should be carefully chosen to suit the amount of light available. Remember that you will need a source of water to irrigate the plantings, to maintain any water feature and to keep the space clean. Electricity may be required for lighting or for any water pumps, but neither of these is essential for a successful courtyard garden.

Typical features of a courtyard garden:

- sliding screens, small fence panels and bamboo blinds for private areas;

- dry-garden elements with one or two rocks and a "pool" of raked gravel;

- stone paving bordered by lanterns;

- stepping stones;

- clipped evergreens such as azaleas, mahonias, nandinas and bamboos;

- glossy evergreen shrubs, such as aucubas, fatsias and camellias, as well as shade-loving ferns, bamboos and farfugiums;

- a carpeting of moss;

- lanterns, basins and small bridges.

CLASSIC FEATURES & ELEMENTS

A common impression of the Japanese garden is that it is decked out with lanterns, curved red bridges, basins and bamboo fences. Indeed, man-made constructs add form and scale to a garden and, when used well with the natural elements of rocks and water, can contribute to its beauty and overall aesthetic. There are hundreds of designs for fences, lanterns and water basins, and each artefact is designed to bring the best out of the space and overall form of a typical garden. From an elaborate dry water construction to the simplest of water basins, the decorative features of a Japanese garden are arguably its most important elements. This chapter examines the classic features of a traditional Japanese garden, including rocks, sand and gravel; ponds; dry water; stepping-stones and *tsukubai*.

Left *This understated composition at Koto-in, Kyoto, illustrates just how little is needed to conjure a perfectly serene atmosphere.*

Rocks & boulders

Rocks have formed the foundation of the Japanese garden from its earliest days. No other culture has made rocks so central to its garden art. It is possible to trace the history of the placement of rocks from their first use in shrines and later as motifs for sacred mountains, to their grouping in and around water. Later, in the dry gardens of the Muromachi period (1393–1568), water was replaced by sand, while in the gardens of the Edo period (1603–1867) rocks were replaced by clipped shrubs, which were used to imitate hills and mountains.

Rocks were originally thought to possess spirits and the ability to draw the gods down to earth. They were later used to represent the mountain homes of the Immortals, as well as the Buddha and his attendants.

Below *The scale and quantity of these rocks at Nijo Castle were intended to express the power of Ieyasu Tokugawa (1543–1616) in the early 1600s.*

However, Zen monks, who had little time for superstition, rejected much of the esoteric symbolism of rocks and gave them more philosophical and decorative roles.

Although rocks were, and still are, placed in symbolic groups, they now tend to be arranged according to certain aesthetic rules. It takes a well-trained and experienced eye to read the symbolism in a group of stones. Groups of rocks that appear entirely natural may actually possess a number of possible symbolic meanings. Therein lies the genius of the Japanese rock-setters. However, do not let this put you off creating symbolic arrangements in your own garden. Historians and Zen practitioners may like to read complex messages in classic rock arrangements, but it is not necessary to have such a deep understanding to compose successful groupings. It was, after all, the study of Chinese and Japanese minimalist ink-and-brush paintings that inspired them.

Above *At Konchi-in, in Kyoto, the viewer is drawn to the rocks in the centre of a layered composition.*

Opposite *Even when used symbolically, rocks are set in a way that is sympathetic to their natural desires.*

Rocks are generally placed in groups. Seven was an auspicious number to the Chinese, as it is in many cultures, and was the original number of the Mystic Isles. Most groups will consist of one main stone and up to five accessory stones, with one or more unifying stones to stabilize the group. Others may be used as linking stones to join together the members of one group. These stones should respond to the energy of the main stone in one of the following seven ways:

Receptive A rock that is placed to receive the energy from the main stone that is leaning towards it.
Transmitting An attendant rock that transmits energy from the main stone towards others in the group.
Pulling A rock that is angled to counteract a main stone that leans away from it.
Pursuing Set behind a main stone that leans away from it, this rock is angled in the same direction.
Stopping An upright main stone is stabilized by an accompanying one.
Attacking The accompanying rock leans towards a neutral, upright main stone.
Flowing This rock is a passive conductor rather than a more active transmitter; often flat, it acts as a kind of conduit to others.

Types of rock & gravel

Whether you're planning a naturalistic stream garden, a Zen-influenced dry garden *(kare-sansui)* or a small courtyard, rock elements will have a profound influence on the finished look and feel of the space.

Weathered stone
Stone that shows signs of weathering, or of mosses, is particularly valued in Japanese gardens of all kinds. This type of natural weathering is more marked in softer, porous rock types, such as limestone, which absorb moisture.

Rocks for water features
Harder rocks like granite, schist and slate tend to weather slowly, but this can be advantageous in and around

Below *A toad lily* (Tricyrtis) *by a cobble-bottomed stream.*

water features. Large, rounded boulders work very well for natural stream features since they have a water-worn quality and always combine pleasingly with cobbles and pebbles.

Rocks for dry gardens
Slate and schist shear in thin layers, producing pieces with dramatic, jagged outlines – ideal for mountainous "islands" in dry gardens. Slate may be very dark when wet with rain and is a particularly good choice for more abstract arrangements.

Paving
Pathways through the Japanese garden can be made from different kinds of stone, from new or man-made paving stones to reclaimed stone from various sources. Stepping stones are often used in water features or gravel areas.

Random paving
This kind of paving, using irregularly cut stone pieces, is popular in Japanese gardens. The stone needs careful laying to accommodate pieces of varying thickness and to minimize the width of mortar joints. Kerbstones and stone setts are also

Above *Stepping stones with roof tiles dividing two kinds of gravel.*

used to define pathways and to separate areas of differing colour, pattern or function.

Reclaimed stones
Paving that is reclaimed, with a rough-hewn look or with worn or weathered surfaces, is much sought after. Japanese gardeners will often incorporate pieces once used for other purposes, such as original millstones and worn stone door lintels or steps.

Stepping stones
A very common feature of Japanese gardens, stepping stones are used in both wet and dry locations. A zig-zagging pathway might artfully combine rounded stepping stones

Above *This path is made up of a mixture of cobbles, paving and a temple pillar base.*

with rectangular elements, often also mingled with cobbles or pebbles. Handcrafted granite stepping stones, broadly circular and with softly bevelled edges, are laid following age-old patterns.

Natural paving stone

Certain types of sedimentary rock can be split very easily along the overlying layers, making them ideal contenders for paving. These include pale grey or creamy coloured limestone, which often has visible remnants of fossilized organisms and shells. Sandstones are also used for paving. Granite is traditional in Japanese gardens and is one of the most resistant stones to wear and tear. Slate is another excellent paving option, although pieces tend to be cut relatively thinly, so they must be laid on a full mortar bed to give adequate support. Often used for pathways, the smooth, rounded surfaces of cobbles, pebbles and paddlestones make a pleasing contrast to regular paving slabs or flat stepping stones.

Cobbles

Acting as a helpful transition from large rounded boulders to smaller pebbles, cobbles tend to be required in relatively small quantities for ordinary domestic garden schemes. Some cobbles are relatively unmarked but range in colour from white, through brown, red and grey to almost black, reflecting different rock types.

Pebbles

In nature, pebbles often represent a wide mixture of rock types, fragments of which have been worn smooth and rounded by the action of water or ice. When wet, they glisten and may show an extraordinary range of colours, flecks and stripes.

Paddlestones

These flat or paddle-shaped pieces of stone with gently rounded edges come in sizes from 15cm (6in) across to as much as 60cm (24in). Although they are sometimes used for ground cover and for creating interesting surface textures, these stones are ideal for representing a stream because the pieces can be laid to overlap and "flow" in the direction of the imaginary water.

Sand and fine grit

A well-known feature of many Japanese gardens is an area of sand or fine grit, raked into swirling patterns to represent forms in nature. This can be a practical option for a newly created Japanese garden if thought is given to the materials, location, and the size of the area within the garden.

Coarse grit and gravel

Gravel is a relatively inexpensive ground cover when compared to paving. When laid over landscape membrane, it can also be surprisingly low maintenance. Finer gravels may also be used as an alternative around rock formations in a dry Zen garden.

Below *The waves of these two sand seas "interrupt" each other.*

Dry water

The original dry landscape gardens focused on the placement of rocks in moss or grass. In later dry gardens, rocks were set in sand, gravel and among pebbles, with these elements arranged and spread to imitate the qualities of water: either as a stream, when on a flat surface, or as a waterfall, when carefully constructed on a slope. One of the most important parts of a dry waterfall design is the high stones at the back, representing the waterfall height. It can then end in a dry stream or pond when it reaches the foot of the slope.

The first two great gardens with rocks set in grass or moss were the 14th-century Saiho-ji, or Moss Temple, and Tenryu-ji. At the latter there is the superb Dragon Gate Waterfall, created with all the power of a real, flowing waterfall. At the Saiho-ji, there is a large turtle representation and a hillside with dramatic arrangements of rocks. The Zen Buddhist monks who created such dry gardens realized that the imagination is more captivated by a suggestion than by reality. Or, as they might have put it, the power of the imagined shape yields a far greater truth than one locked up in the actual. This is what is meant by the poetic term *yugen*, or "the spirit of hidden depth". Streams, as opposed to still water, are portrayed in their "dry" form by the use of river-washed pebbles laid out carefully in overlapping patterns to indicate a sense of flow. The image is completed by the use of a few larger boulders or rocks, as well as bridges made of large stone slabs.

There is great potential for contemporary designers to use a dry rock-and-sand garden to create even more abstract patterns, using quarry-blasted rocks rather than naturally occurring weathered stones. This takes the "suggestive" nature of the dry landscape into the realm of contemporary design. Not all modern Japanese garden designers follow Zen precepts; they have become more Western in outlook. However, the overall design of these modern gardens remains essentially Japanese.

Opposite *At Tofukuji, in Kyoto, the 20th-century artist-designer Mirei Shigemori used sand to imitate water, recalling ocean waves lapping at island shores.*

Below *At Konchi-in, various symbolic forms are depicted with rocks and pines, surrounded by fine white gravel to represent the sea.*

Plants & topiary

The "hard" elements of a garden – gravel, rocks and architectural features – are important in Japanese landscape design. However, "soft" elements – plants, trees and shrubs – are also vital.

A necessary ingredient in most Japanese gardens for ground cover, moss requires the right balance of sun and shade to grow well. The variety of different species of moss gives the surface of the garden a beautiful velvety texture in all shades of green, often highlighted by the dappled sun if the moss is growing beneath trees. The advantage of growing moss rather than grass is that it gives the designer much more freedom in terms of positioning plants, as it does not need to be mown in the same way as grass. Similarly, plants are not used as much as in Western gardens, yet when they are used they are not simply a design element but often hold symbolic significance too. So most Japanese gardens will contain one or more of the most symbolic plants, such as plum (symbolising purity), cherry (mortality) or maple (longevity). Although Japan's mountains, streams and coastlines are brimming with superb flora, the disciplined restraint of Japanese gardens focuses on certain types of plants. The native plant area in Kyoto's botanical garden is full of plants that Western gardeners would relish, but most of them would not find a home in a Japanese garden.

In terms of planting style, most shrubs in the Japanese garden are set out in random, natural-looking groups or as individual specimens. Formal, symmetrical styles are rarely used, and shrubs and flowers are not planted for their textures or colours. In tea gardens, you will find plants such as ferns that lend a wild quality to the design. In stark contrast, other gardens are planted with clipped evergreens, in which groups of shrubs, usually azaleas and camellias, are clipped into abstract topiary shapes. Indeed, topiary has been part of the way the Japanese have represented the abstraction of nature in their gardens since the earliest gardens of the Nara and Heian periods. In the most famous traditional Japanese gardens, there are very few examples of the kind of "cloud pruning" that you often find in copies of Japanese gardens, especially

Left *The dry garden of Shoden-ji uses clipped azaleas instead of rocks. The azaleas are planted in the same 5-3-2-5 arrangement that was used for placing rocks in the 15th and 16th centuries throughout temple gardens.*

in the USA, where all kinds of plants, from juniper to boxwood, are clipped into a series of rounded "cloud" forms. These sculptured plants can be spectacular but can also, in the wrong setting, look rather comical. In the same way that the Japanese enjoy the simple and natural form of rocks while the Chinese enjoy eccentric and convoluted shapes, Japanese garden designers also use their version of topiary with sensitivity and restraint. In the 16th and 17th centuries this practice of *o-karikomi* (Japanese topiary) reached its peak of artistry. With care, it can be utilized in a Japanese garden in any of the main styles, using all kinds of plants.

The man acknowledged as the master of *o-karikomi* was Kobori Enshu (1579–1647). A soldier, town planner, tea-master and garden designer, Enshu introduced the clipping of great masses of evergreens, most often blocks of azaleas but using mixed plantings too, shaping them into abstract forms that suggested the movement of waves, the folding of hill ranges, and even, in the garden of Daichi-ji near Kyoto, a treasure-ship on an ocean. In the temple garden of Raikyu-ji, in Takahashi, Enshu combined the art of *o-karikomi* with the art of *shakkei*, clipping blocks of azaleas into forms that, in one part of the garden, imitate ocean waves around the Mystic Isles of the Immortals, while in another the forms echo and draw in the outline of the surrounding hills. The overall effect makes for a brilliant composition.

Below *A pagoda-style lantern provides the central focus of the entire garden at Sanzen-in. The mixed hedge curves up a hillside of randomly placed, clipped azaleas. This kind of topiary in Japan is known as* o-karikomi.

Decorative artefacts

In the Japanese garden, specimen plants, focal points, sculptures and statues are usually shunned, as are overt colour schemes, textural combinations, surprise effects and most of the elements that are the bedrock of many Western gardens. This general emphasis also incorporates more religious sculptural forms such as stupas, pagodas, water basins, lanterns or images of the Buddha. Although these artefacts are still integral to modern Japanese gardens, their religious significance can be more diluted.

Pagodas and stupas are structures of the Buddhist treasure houses where relics and scriptures were stored to commemorate a saint. Like lanterns, they were found close to temples, but when used in the garden they do not dominate because they are such familiar images that they readily blend into the scene. There are, however, one or two playful devices found in Japanese gardens that recall a distant rural past. Deer scarers (*shishi-odoshi*) are the best known of these. They use water to make a noise intended to startle any deer feeding on plants in the garden. A more unusual device is the *sui-kinkutsu* ("water harp chamber") which projects the sound of water dripping in an underground chamber. Wells may also be found in Japanese gardens, constructed of timber or natural stone, and often with a bamboo rack as a cover to prevent leaves from falling in. The use of wells, whether real or decorative, is common in conjunction with tea gardens to indicate a pure source of water for making tea.

Below, from left *A stone pagoda in a grove of the rare Chinese fir* (Cunninghamia lanceolata)*; a statue of the Buddha; lanterns may be placed on promontories as the watchful symbol of a lighthouse.*

Lighting

There is a large selection of garden lights available, from tiny concealed uplighters made to highlight individual plants or rocks, to Japanese-style lanterns, which are among the most distinctive sculptural artefacts in the Japanese garden. Originally these lanterns stood outside Shinto shrines and Buddhist temples, sometimes in their hundreds, lining up in avenues of flickering lights. Like other artefacts such as the water basin and the stepping-stone path, lanterns found their way into the Japanese garden by way of the tea garden. They were originally placed to illuminate tea paths and water basins, as many tea gatherings were arranged in the evening. They were also placed near pond edges to represent lighthouses, or at the base of slopes or near wells. Despite their popularity, stone lanterns (with oil and wick lamps or candles placed inside) did not give much light and were, to a large extent, ornamental.

Above, from left *A stone lantern used to light the path leading to a tea garden and water basins; brushwood, reeds, timber posts and bamboo are all combined in this sleeve fence, which stands at the corner of a house and helps divide up the garden; a* tsukubai, *or water basin, accompanied by a lantern, is placed outside a tea-house.*

Sculpted ornaments are rare in Japanese gardens, so stone lanterns, especially granite ones, give an opportunity to create something interesting and distinctive. Brand new granite lanterns are often bright silvery grey and the colour can be too startling. It can take many years before granite weathers naturally to give that patina or aged effect that is evoked in the term *wabi-sabi*. The term has no literal translation, but roughly means "withered loneliness", and became an essential part of the tea ceremony philosophy. When applied to ornaments, it implies the patina of age.

Streams, waterfalls & ponds

In the past, streams would have been used on ceremonial occasions in Japan as settings for poetry readings and for drinking tea and saki. They would typically lead in and out of shallow ponds, often home to both koi and common carp. Ponds were also combined with small islands, and a pine tree on an island is one of the classic images of Japan. The bridges that cross from the mainland to the island give a good view of the fish and flowers in the shallow water. Waterfalls are the third water element, believed by Japanese gardeners to be best placed for reflecting the moon. This stunning effect can be recreated in your garden as long as you take care to place the waterfall so that it looks as natural as possible.

The first Japanese gardens of the Nara and early Heian periods had winding streams that bordered the courtyard before feeding the main pond. These were often edged with rocks, the two forming an important relationship. A grand stone might be used to mark the headwater of the stream as it entered the garden. Other rocks would "follow the desire" of this stone, responding to its position and shape, forcing the water this way and that, changing its mood as it approached the pond. Mountainside, torrent-style streams required the scattering of many more random stones, which caused the stream to divide and flow rapidly through narrowing channels. A *yarimizu* is a meandering stream of the type that might be found flowing through a meadow, and it can be used in gardens to create a wetland area, including an estuary planted with reeds and irises – popular in the Japanese garden.

Waterfalls are an essential feature of pond and stream gardens and also of stroll gardens. They are often built to represent the Buddhist Trinity, with one large stone at the centre, over which the water tumbles, supported on either side by two attendant stones that stand slightly further forward. Large and important waterfalls were often known as dragon-gate waterfalls after the Chinese symbol for waterfall, which included a dragon and water. A stone might be placed at the waterfall's base to represent a carp, as if it were about to leap. This "carp stone" symbolized spiritual and mental endeavour in Buddhist and Confucian terms.

Whether it moves through a stream or waterfall, the water needs eventually to flow into a pond. In Japanese gardens, ponds tend to be no deeper than 45cm (18in) so

Left *A natural and artistic waterfall is the centrepiece of this peaceful stroll garden.*

that they are easily kept clean and clear, and the fish can be seen. The proposed layout of the pond edges will determine what happens to the water. For example, the water might appear to lap against a rocky shoreline, with a few solitary stones jutting out into the water, or it could become a wide inlet bordered by a sand bar. One sand-bar scene – the Aminoshidate peninsula in western Honshu – is so famous that it is cited as one of the three most important landscapes in Japan. It is frequently symbolically reproduced in Japanese gardens, often shown with a lantern on a promontory to represent a lighthouse. The shapes of ponds should, wherever possible, recall a natural scene, perhaps even the seaside or an island.

Islands in Japanese gardens might reproduce special scenes, such as the hundreds of extraordinary rocky islets in Matsushima Bay, near Sendai, in northern Honshu. Some of these islands are very small, but most have some kind of plant life, particularly pines, growing in their rocky crevices. Apart from the pine-covered islands, there are other styles, including the Rocky Islet, Meadow Island, Forest Island and Cove Beach Island. These islands were originally placed towards the middle of the pond, but slightly off-centre, to create a sense of mystery so that, whether you were boating or walking, you might discover an inlet, waterfall, grotto, or even another island behind them.

Below *A lantern sits on a promontory playing the role of a lighthouse. The flowering grass is* Miscanthus, *a native of Japan where it grows in waste ground.*

Below *This curving slab of schist in the grounds of Nijo Castle is a potent symbol of strength. The original garden was thought to have been designed as a dry garden.*

Tsukubai

Some Japanese gardens contain very distinctive water features called *tsukubai*, or water basins. These water basins were often found in traditional tea gardens and were used for providing drinking water. They were usually fed by a natural spring. Taller basins, *chozubachi*, are sited nearer the house. Another traditional Japanese water feature, the *shishi-odoshi*, was designed as a deer scarer and uses running water to make a knocking noise with a bamboo pole against a stone basin, a sound loud enough to deter marauding animals from eating tender plants in the garden.

You will often find a water basin or other standing water feature in a Japanese garden, and sometimes even two or three such features. Water basins are not always

Below *A water basin filling from a water pipe hidden inside tubes of bamboo.*

kept full, except those that are fed from a concealed bamboo pipe that is allowed to drip into the basin to keep the water fresh, rippling and constantly overflowing. Water basins that are not automatically filled will need cleaning out and topping up with fresh water. In addition, just as the path can be cleaned and damped down before the guests arrive, the sides of stone water basins may also be wetted to darken and intensify the natural colours and markings of the stone. The water basin itself may be a simple rounded bowl carved from a single piece of granite, but traditional designs (copied from various historic shrines and temples in Japan) vary, and some are surprisingly geometric, cube-shaped or cylindrical, with carved patterns and designs around the outside. These intricate designs tend to stand out more than the rustic bowls, making a pleasing contrast to the surrounding rock forms and plantings. Nowadays, materials other than granite are often used, and the more porous they are, the more quickly they will develop a pleasing patina of age due to the moist environment.

Chozubachi basins are usually slightly taller – up to 1m (3ft) high – and are placed on verandas where they can easily be reached from the house. These basins may have a slatted bamboo cover to keep the water fresh, to stop birds from drinking there and to prevent leaves and debris from falling in. *Furisode* basins come in the form of a narrow, naturally rippled rock that is shaped like the long sleeve of a kimono. A bowl is carved into the stone, sometimes in the shape of a gourd. Conversely, the *tsukubai chozubachi* is a low, or crouching, basin placed on or just off the *roji* (the path to the tea house). The act of crouching to reach the basin, like the bending needed for the middle crawl-through gate and the tea house's small hatch-like entrance, compels guests to be humble.

Above *A water basin in the Seiryu tea garden at Nijo Castle garden. The gourd-shaped rock is a symbol of hospitality.*

Above *The* tsukubai, *or "crouching basin," one of the most symbolic features of the Japanese garden.*

Above *A 17th-century tsukubai in the temple of Ryoan-ji, with an inscription that means "I learn only to be contented," an important goal of Zen philosophy.*

Above Generally, *water basins are constantly filled by fresh water, the excess draining away among rocks and pebbles.*

DIRECTORY OF PLANTS

Although initially many plants were imported from China, Japanese gardeners soon harnessed the potential of their native plants. Japan has exceptional and enviable flora, including many species of cherry, azalea, camellia and magnolia, which blossom in the mountains in spring, while in the autumn, maples and oaks give a display of fiery reds, yellows and oranges. Evergreen trees such as cedars and pines are considered symbols of longevity and resilience.

Wisterias, peonies and hydrangeas feature in many Japanese gardens, in natural groupings or massed in orchard-like groves rather than in formal beds. Herbaceous and bulbous plants, such as platycodons, lilies, hostas or Japanese anemones, are usually planted naturalistically with ferns in individual clumps near the base of a rock, in a carpet of moss, or scattered in small groups. Irises are grown in swampy areas or in formal beds near the inlet of a pond, while sedges and ferns are used to soften the edges of streams.

Left *In the autumn the leaves of the Japanese maple (Acer palmatum) turn an amazing mixture of flame tones.*

Spring

Camellia japonica
Tsubaki
CAMELLIA
Family: THEACEAE

This evergreen shrub, native to the warm temperate coasts of Japan, is planted in gardens together with species and hybrids from China. *Camellia sasanqua* has smaller, narrower leaves than *C. japonica*, and the pale pink single flowers appear sporadically through winter before dropping when spent. Camellias are now common, but in the past they were found mainly in Buddhist temples. The simpler, paler coloured, single-flowered forms with glossy foliage,

Camellia japonica

known as *wabi-suke*, were planted in tea gardens. Two types of camellia can be grown as hedges: the dense, glossy foliage of *C. japonica,* or the tea plant *C. sinensis*, with smaller leaves than other species and white flowers in autumn, often clipped to give a compact, dense shape.
Propagation semi-ripe leaf cuttings
Flowering time mid- to late spring
Size shrub or small tree to 10m (30ft); keep to 2m (6½ft) by restricting the roots in a tub, or by regular stem pruning
Pruning by thinning out stems after flowering
Conditions light shade and away from early morning sun; moist, acid soil
Fully hardy/Z 6–7

Kerria japonica
Yamabuki
JEW'S MALLOW
Family: ROSACEAE

A deciduous shrub native to Japan, kerria has been

grown in gardens since the 11th century. Its simple, five-petalled, orange-yellow, star-like flowers are a welcome sight in spring. The double-flowered form is most common in the West, but Japanese gardens tend to use the single form.
Propagation hardwood cuttings
Flowering time mid- to late spring
Size shrub to 2m (6½ft)
Pruning by thinning out old stems after flowering
Conditions full sun or partial shade; any soil
Fully hardy/Z 5–9

Magnolia spp.
Mokuren
MAGNOLIA
Family: MAGNOLIACEAE

Native magnolias include the deep purple-pink, lily-flowered *Magnolia liliflora*, known as *mokuren;* the familiar white, star-flowered *M. stellata*, *hime-kobushi;* and its taller close relative, *M. kobus*, *kobushi.* The large

Magnolia stellata

M. obovata, to 15m (50ft), is a hardy, deciduous tree with highly scented, cream-coloured flowers in midsummer. In more recent years the bold American evergreen species, *M. grandiflora* (bull bay), growing to 18m (60ft), has proved popular, with its large, cream-coloured flowers appearing in late summer.
Propagation seed and grafted
Flowering time mid-spring to midsummer
Size large shrub or small tree, 3–12m (10–40ft)
Pruning by removing over-long shoots in late winter; best left unpruned
Conditions partial shade; rich, acid soil
Fully hardy/Z 5–9

Paulownia tomentosa
Kiri
FOXGLOVE TREE
Family: SCROPHULARIACEAE
Although strictly a native of China, the foxglove tree has been cultivated in Japan since the 9th century. Planted as specimen trees in the courtyard gardens of aristocrats, they became associated with the military leader, Hideyoshi. *Paulownias* have two notable features: the fabulously large leaves and the beautiful, lavender-blue, foxglove-shaped flowers. It may take a few years and some mild winters before a *Paulownia* will establish a strong stem, but once a trunk has developed, the tree will form a handsome and perfectly hardy crown. Alternatively, the stems may be coppiced in spring to encourage the production of massive leaves, up to a metre (40in) wide. This eliminates the flowers, but when combined with bamboos, palms and cycads, it has a bold, tropical look.

Paulownia tomentosa

Propagation seed
Flowering time mid- to late spring
Size tree to 12m (40ft)
Pruning none needed unless grown as a pollard
Conditions sheltered position in full sun; any soil
Fully hardy/Z 6–9

Prunus persica
Momo
PEACH
Family: ROSACEAE
The deciduous Japanese peach is the next flowering tree, after the plum, to be honoured in spring. Peach blossom is a soft, vibrant pink, and the flowers appear just as the leaves unfurl. The peach was thought to win over the spirits of the dead, and was also a sign of new life. Concoctions of peach were taken at the first sign of pregnancy and were administered as a cure for morning sickness. Peach trees are generally rather short-lived (as little as 15 years) and are prey to a number of pests and diseases, including the disfiguring peach leaf curl.

Propagation budded or grafted
Flowering time early spring
Size tree to 8m (25ft)
Pruning by removing dead, diseased and damaged branches in midsummer
Conditions full sun; rich, well-drained soil
Fully hardy/Z 7–9

Prunus serrulata
Sakura
JAPANESE CHERRY
Family: ROSACEAE
The classic Japanese cherries mostly date from the late 19th-century Meiji period. These trees often have fully double and profuse blossoms that derive from the Japanese hill cherry, *Prunus serrulata*. The best-loved forms are those with white flowers and dark, unfurling leaves that are revealed as the petals fall.

The first of the cherries to flower, from late autumn to spring, is *P.* x *subhirtella* (Higan cherry, rosebud cherry). Its weeping forms, 'Pendula Rosea' and 'Pendula Rosea Plena', are very popular in Japan, the cascading branches being propped up by cedar poles and bamboo frames. *P. incisa* flowers soon after, just before its leaves appear, and makes a small, spreading, attractive tree to 8m (25ft), ideal for the smaller garden. The next to flower is the hybrid *P.* x *yedoensis* (Yoshino cherry), named after Mount Yoshino. The white flowers appear just as the leaves break from their buds, and the spreading tree has a lovely, weeping form, 'Shidare-yoshino'.
Propagation budded or grafted
Flowering time early to late spring
Size tree 3–8m (10–25ft)
Pruning by removing dead, diseased and damaged branches in midsummer
Conditions full sun; rich, well-drained soil
Fully hardy/Z 7–9

Summer

Clematis spp.
Tessen
CLEMATIS
Family: RANUNCULACEAE
Some species of large-flowered clematis, such as *C. patens*, are native to Japan. Although rarely grown as climbers over arbours as they are in Western gardens, the very colourful hybrids of *C. patens* are often planted in containers and placed near the main house entrance.
Propagation seed, all cuttings, layers
Flowering time summer
Size climber up to 4m (13ft)
Conditions sun and part shade
Fully hardy/Z 4–9

Hydrangea
Ajisai
HYDRANGEA
Family: HYDRANGEACEAE
Hydrangeas were first mentioned in Japanese gardens as early as AD759, but they did not become instantly popular. The four petals and rather gloomy purple colours were thought to represent death. The common name, *ajisai*, means "to gather purple". They were also called *shichihenge*, which meant "to change seven times", alluding to the way in which the flower colour alters through the season. Three of the most important species of hydrangea are native to Japan: *Hydrangea macrophylla*, *H. petiolaris* (climbing hydrangea) and *H. serrata*. The great round mop-head hybrids originated here and are found in a number of Japanese gardens. Among their useful attributes are their late-summer flowering and their ability to withstand heavy summer downpours. On acid soil with plenty of moisture, the blue varieties are intensely blue. The lacecaps, which come closer to the species in their flower form, are also very elegant and suitable for planting in light woodland shade, where their mysterious beauty can be almost bewitching, especially when the flowers are moist from the rain. Varieties of *H. macrophylla* can be grown in pots, if regularly fed and watered. The other species that is native to Japan is *H. paniculata*, which has cone-shaped flowerheads in late summer. It is ultra-hardy and can be grown in full sun. All these hydrangeas come in a multitude of forms to suit every taste, and they have become very popular in Japan in recent years, with some towns and districts making

Hydrangea

the hydrangea their special flower.
Propagation semi-ripe and hardwood cuttings
Flowering time mid- to late summer
Size shrub to 2m (6½ft)
Pruning by removing dead and over-long shoots in early spring
Conditions sun or partial shade; moist, rich soil
Fully hardy/Z 4–9

Ipomoea
Asagao
MORNING GLORY
Family: CONVOLVULACEAE
During the Nara and Heian periods, when poets typically sang of the fleeting condition of human life, they latched on to morning glory as an ideal symbol: as one flower fades after a day of glory, it is quickly replaced by another. But it was in the 18th and 19th centuries that the morning glory became fashionable among the *daimyos*, who helped to create a new array of colours. Morning glory is usually grown in

pots over lightweight bamboo trellises and fences. While so many flowers tend to wilt at the onset of summer, the morning glory revels in the heat.

Propagation seed
Flowering time summer to autumn
Size climber to 6m (20ft)
Conditions full sun; any soil
Tender/Z 8–10

Iris spp.
Hanashobu
IRIS
Family: IRIDACEAE
The iris is a great favourite in Japan. *Iris laevigata*, known as *kakitsubata*, grows naturally in the swamps around the ancient capital of Nara, where it was collected to be made into a dye, its blue colour exclusively used to decorate the robes of the imperial family. *I. laevigata* is cultivated in gardens in swampy, but not waterlogged, ground, often near an inlet to a pond. *Yatsuhashi* or zigzag plank bridges weave over the beds,

Iris laevigata

forcing the visitor to slow down and admire the plants from different angles. The flowers are narrower and smaller than the larger and flatter *I. ensata* var. *spontanea*, known as *hanashobu*. *Hanashobu* is more spectacular than *kakitsubata* and has been bred intensively. It now comes in all shapes and colours, from deep purple to white and pink, and is often cultivated in large beds in slightly ridged rows or in pots, so that it can be admired as an individual against golden folding screens. Other irises grown are the shade-loving *I. japonica* and *I.tectorum* (roof iris).

Propagation division
Flowering time summer
Size to 80cm (32in)

Conditions full sun or partial shade; slightly acid soil
Fully hardy/Z 4–9

Nelumbo nucifera
Hana-basu
LOTUS
Family: NYMPHAEACEAE
The lotus symbolizes the evolution of the human spirit, with its roots in the mud, its growth passing through water and air and into the sun, to open its flowers, pure and unsullied. A succession of flowers appear over six weeks, the buds opening at dawn with an indescribable sound. The white flowers of *N. nucifera* 'Alba' have an especially powerful and sweet perfume. Lotus flowers close in the heat of the day and after a couple of days gracefully fall, one petal at a time, leaving their distinctive honeycombed seed pods. The lotus is also an important source of nourishment. The seeds, roots and leaves are all eaten, but varieties grown as food rarely flower.

Propagation division
Flowering time summer
Size 1.2m (4ft) above water
Conditions full sun; in water to a depth of 60cm (24in)
Half Hardy/Z 4–11

Spiraea nipponica
Shimotsuke
NIPPON SPIRAEA
Family: ROSACEAE
Several species of spiraea are native to Japan, most small to medium-sized shrubs. They make a round or spreading shape, with arching growth, decked with bunches of tiny flowers.

Propagation semi-ripe cuttings
Flowering time midsummer
Size shrub to 1.2m (4ft)
Pruning by cutting back after flowering
Conditions full sun; any soil
Fully Hardy/Z 5-9

Nelumbo nucifera

Autumn

Acer palmatum
Kaede
JAPANESE MAPLE
Family: ACERACEAE
The Japanese maple is perhaps second only to the cherry blossom in popularity in Japan, and it has become a tradition to take special trips to view the flaming autumn tints of their wild maples. *Acer palmatum* is native to Japan, where it can be seen mingling on hillsides with cedars, bamboos and pines. Although there are hundreds of varieties of Japanese maple, some with finely cut leaves and others with variegated, or purple foliage, the species *A. palmatum* is the chief focus of all the celebrations in gardens and in the wild. *A. micranthum*, *A. tataricum* var. *ginnala* and *A. japonicum* are also native, and all turn beautiful colours, but in November the temples and gardens of Kyoto are ablaze with the fiery red and orange leaves of *A. palmatum*. Some very beautiful forms of Japanese maple have foliage that is salmon-tinted in spring, while some turn bright yellow rather than red in autumn, and others have bright red or green stems in winter. The dwarf and cut-leaf forms may be more suitable for the smaller garden, but it is better to try and avoid the purple-leaf forms, which tend to distract from carefully composed, harmonious arrangements.
Propagation seed and grafted (all named varieties will need to be

Acer palmatum

grafted, although to raise just one or two plants you can layer them).
Size small tree to 8m (25ft)
Pruning best left unpruned; can cut out over-long stems in late winter
Conditions full sun or partial shade; moist soil; occasionally the young growth can be injured by late frosts or cold winds
Fully hardy/Z 5–8

Acer buergerianum
Buerger-kaede
TRIDENT MAPLE
Family: ACERACEAE
This small oval tree is often seen in larger Japanese gardens, but in a mild autumn holds on to its leaves well into the winter, and will not always colour as reliably as some of the other species. It has a multi-stemmed habit and medium-fine, glossy dark green leaves. The bark exfoliates to expose an orangish under-bark.

Acer buergerianum

Acer cissifolium
Mitsude-kaede
IVY-LEAVED MAPLE
Family: ACERACEAE
This barely looks like a maple at all with its three-lobed leaves. It is one of the very first to colour in autumn, but keeps those leaves for a remarkably long time as they turn a patchwork of oranges, yellows and reds.

Anemone spp.
Shummeigiku
ANEMONE
Family: RANUNCULACEAE
Plants known as Japanese anemones have been developed from the Chinese import *Anemone hupehensis*, which has been

extensively hybridized. This tall herbaceous plant with vine-like leaves is often seen in shady gardens, planted in clumps of moss and beside streams. The finest form is the single, pure white *A.* x *hybrida* 'Honorine Jobert', but there are many cultivars, with colours ranging from white and pale pink to a deep purple-pink, some with double flowers. In fertile soil it can be invasive and may need to be kept under control.
Propagation division
Flowering time late summer to mid-autumn
Size perennial to 1.2m (4ft)
Conditions sun or partial shade; rich, moist soil
Fully hardy/Z 5–8

Miscanthus sinensis

Callicarpa japonica
Murasaki shikobu
JAPANESE BEAUTY BERRY
Family: VERBENACEAE
Named after the author of the great 11th-century novel *The Tale of Genji*, the Japanese species *Callicarpa japonica* (beauty berry) is a low-growing, arching, deciduous shrub, which bears beautiful purple berries in autumn and winter. It has delicate pink flowers that arrive in the early summer (preceding the purple berries) and simple, medium blue-green leaves. Its larger cousin, *C. bodinieri* var. *bodinieri* 'Profusion', is more frequently planted in Western gardens but is a much larger shrub.
Propagation semi-ripe cuttings
Flowering time late summer
Size shrub to 1.5m (5ft)
Pruning cut back close to ground level in early spring
Conditions sun or light shade; rich soil
Fully hardy/Z 5–8

Tricyrtis

Miscanthus sinensis
Obana, susuki
FOUNTAIN GRASS OR
EULALIA GRASS
Family: POACEAE
Because *Miscanthus sinensis* colonizes waste ground in Japan it is rarely used as a garden plant. When it is, it is used with restraint. The silvery plumes, which appear in autumn, reach 2–4m (7–13ft) high. *M. sinensis* 'Yakushima Dwarf' is a low-growing form from Yakushima, the volcanic island off the south coast of Japan, which makes a rounded clump 1m (3ft) high and across. The old flower and leaf stems turn to shades of fawn, persisting into the New Year before being dispersed by the wind. Eulalia grass covers many of the hills in Japan,

where it waves elegantly in the wind.
Propagation division
Flowering time autumn
Size grass to 4m (13ft)
Conditions full sun; well-drained soil
Fully hardy/Z 5–9

Tricyrtis
Hototogisu
TOAD LILY
Family: CONVALLARIACEAE
The old Chinese name for this plant translates as "oil spot plant" because its flowers are freckled with spots. Its Japanese name, *hototogisu*, is the same as the name for a cuckoo, which has a freckled chest. This genus, known in the West as toad lily, has only recently become popular in Japan, where its wild forms with their modest and mysterious colours are suitable for planting in moist shade.
Propagation division
Flowering time late summer to mid-autumn
Size perennial to 80cm (32in)
Conditions shade; rich, moist soil
Fully hardy/Z 7

Other plants of interest

Althaea rosea
Tachi-oi
HOLLYHOCK
Family: MALVACEAE
The hollyhock has been popular in Japan since Heian times and is still common, especially in gardens of small houses.
Propagation seed
Flowering time early to midsummer
Size perennial to 2.4m (8ft)
Conditions full sun; any soil
Fully hardy/Z 6–9

Cryptomeria japonica
Sugi
JAPANESE CEDAR
Family: TAXODIACEAE
After the pine, the most important and sacred conifer in Japan is the

Cryptomeria japonica

Japanese cedar. This is capable of living for more than 2,000 years and is often planted as a sign of virtue and as a guardian at the entrance of Buddhist and Shinto shrines. Cryptomerias are planted in most of the commercial forests in Japan, as it is an easily worked timber and is used extensively in the building industry. The cryptomeria is a towering, conical tree, with finely dissected, scaly foliage. It is often coppiced in gardens, and the new growth is pruned into tiers with shaped, pompom-like foliage at the ends. There are many cultivated varieties of *C. japonica*, but most are merely curiosities.
Propagation seed, hardwood cuttings
Size tree to 25m (82ft)
Pruning not needed
Conditions full sun or partial shade; deep, moist, slightly acid soil
Fully hardy/Z 6–9

Cycas revoluta
Cycas nana
SAGO PALM
Family: CYCADACEAE
This ancient plant is native to the southern islands of Japan. It is a beautiful glossy evergreen, which looks like a cross between a palm and a fern. It is only marginally hardy, and is rarely seen in gardens north of Kyoto. Even in Kyoto the sago palm has to be wrapped up in winter, and like many other aspects of Japanese gardens, this elaborate wrapping has been raised to the level of an art form.
Propagation seed
Size to 2m (6½ft)
Conditions requires full sun and moist, rich soil.
Half hardy/Z 8–10

Daphniphyllum macropodum
Yuzuri-ha
Family:
DAPHNIPHYLLACEAE
A handsome large-leaved

Hemerocallis

shrub, bearing long strap-like leaves with red leaf stalks. This Japanese native plant, which can be grown in almost any moisture-retentive soil in sun or part shade, makes a good substitute for rhododendrons on alkaline soils where bold foliage is required. It will grow into a large shrub. Its flowers are insignificant but release a pungent scent, producing dark berries in winter.
Propagation seed, semi-ripe cuttings
Flowering time spring
Size shrub to 8m (26ft)
Pruning after flowering, if necessary
Conditions sun or shade
Fully hardy/Z 7–8

Hemerocallis
Kisuge or kanzou
DAY LILY
Family:
HEMEROCALLIDACEAE
H. fulva is native to Japan
and has given rise to
hundreds of varieties. In
its natural state its flowers
are a buff orange, rising up
on stalks in summer from
a deciduous herbaceous
perennial that will colonize
large areas in shade or
full sun. Day lily flowers
last only one day, but a
succession are produced
over several weeks in
mid- to late summer. The
species *H. flava* produces
a lovely fragrance from
its yellow flowers in
the spring.
Propagation division
Flowering time spring to
late summer
Size 90cm (36in)
Conditions sun or shade in
most soil types
Fully hardy/Z 4–8

Phyllostachys aurea
Kosan chiku
FISHPOLE BAMBOO OR
GOLDEN BAMBOO
Family: POACEAE
These mid-green canes

Pinus densiflora

age to golden-brown. It
will spread, so contain
the roots.
Propagation division
Size to 10m (33ft)
Conditions moist soil
and tolerates drought
Hardy/Z 6–8

Phyllostachys edulis
Kina mousou chiku
MOSO BAMBOO
Family: POACEAE
This evergreen bamboo
is often harvested for
its huge stems. In colder
climates it will not
reach its full growth
dimensions, which are
only seen in the southern
half of Japan.
Propagation division
Size to 6m (20ft) or more
Conditions full sun;
medium drought
tolerance, intolerant
of shade
Hardy/Z 7–11

Pinus densiflora
Aka-matsu
JAPANESE RED PINE
Family: PINACEAE
A fine tree with pinkish
red bark and a rounded
head, the Japanese red
pine is often pruned to
accentuate its soft crown
and show its elegant,
branched structure.
Propagation seed, grafted
Size tree to 20m (66ft)
Conditions full sun; any
well-drained soil
Pruning needs little
pruning to develop a
strong structure
Hardy/Z 3–7

Pinus parviflora
Go-yo-matsu
JAPANESE WHITE PINE
Family: PINACEAE
Native to Japan, this type
of pine has shorter, grey-
green needles and is
slower growing and more
manageable than *P.
densiflora* or *P.thunbergii*,
but it will eventually make
a large, multi-stemmed,
mounding tree.
Propagation seed, grafted
Size tree to 20m (66ft)
Conditions full sun; any
well-drained soil

Pruning needs little
pruning to develop a
strong structure.
Hardy/Z 4–7

Rhapis excelsa
Shuro
MINIATURE FAN PALM
Family: ARECACEAE/
PALMAE
Native to China, the
miniature fan palm was
introduced to Japan in the
19th century. With shiny
dark leaves, it is still a
valuable addition to the
tropical look in a temperate
garden. The plant can be
used as group plantation.
It is good for planting in
shaded areas.
Propagation sucker division
Size to 5m (16ft)
Conditions requires a
sheltered position; light
shade and any soil
Fully hardy/Z 8–11

Rhapis excelsa

Index